102 More '

Arkansas

Before You Die

Kea Oburn

Other books by Kat Robinson:

Arkansas Pie: A Delicious Slice of The Natural State
History Press 2012

Classic Eateries of the Ozarks and Arkansas River Valley
History Press 2013

Classic Eateries of the Arkansas Delta
History Press 2014

Another Slice of Arkansas Pie: A Guide to the Best Restaurants, Bakeries, Truck Stops and Food Trucks for Delectable Bites in The Natural State
Tonti Press, March 2018

Arkansas Food: The A to Z of Eating in The Natural State
Tonti Press, December 2018

101 Things To Eat in Arkansas Before You Die
Tonti Press, August 2019

102 More Things to Eat in
Arkansas
Before You Die

A Travel Guide to the Very Best
Plates in The Natural State

Kat Robinson

TONTI
P R E S S

Published by Tonti Press
Little Rock, Arkansas

Cover image of the brisket plate with fried corn on the cob, potato salad
and Texas toast at Blacksheep BBQ in Yellville.

Back cover illustration by the author.

All photography by Kat Robinson except pages 10 (Bavarian Inn),
30 (Steffey's Pizza), and 85 (Shangri-La Resort sandwich and pie),
all by Grav Weldon, with permission.

First published November 2019

Manufactured in the United States of America

ISBN 13: 978-0-9998734-8-9

Library of Congress Control Number:2019949753

No restaurant, bakery, store or other entity paid for inclusion within these
pages. All food photography was taken without manipulation, augmentation
or exaggeration. Every food item is edible and as would be served in each
establishment. The author received no monetary compensation to insert,
rank, or exclude any property in this list.

HERE
is where the adventure
BEGINS.

TABLE OF CONTENTS

- [ ] 28 Springs, Siloam Springs
- [ ] The Bavarian Inn Restaurant, Eureka Springs
- [ ] Catalpa Café, Oark
- [x] CJ's Butcher Boy Burgers, Russellville/Fayetteville
- [ ] Crepes Paulette, Bentonville
- [ ] Dairy Dream, Mountainburg
- [ ] Feltner Brothers, Fayetteville
- [ ] Fork and Crust, Rogers/Fayetteville
- [ ] Fred's Hickory Inn, Bentonville
- [ ] Fried Rice, Fort Smith
- [ ] The Grapevine Restaurant, Paris
- [ ] Grand Taverne, Eureka Springs
- [ ] Grotto Wood-Fired Grill, Eureka Springs
- [ ] Mamma Z's Tortilla Factory, Bentonville
- [ ] Maria's Mexican Restaurant, Fort Smith/ Rogers/Bentonville
- [ ] Mockingbird Kitchen, Fayetteville
- [ ] Mud Street Café, Eureka Springs
- [ ] The Preacher's Son, Bentonville
- [ ] R and R Curry Xpress, Fort Smith/Springdale
- [ ] Rock Café, Waldron
- [ ] Sam's Olde Tyme Hamburgers, Rogers
- [ ] Steffey's Pizza, Lavaca
- [ ] Susan's Restaurant, Springdale
- [ ] Susie Q's Malt Shop, Rogers
- [ ] Tang's Asian Market, Springdale
- [ ] War Eagle Mill, Rogers
- [ ] Wright's Barbecue, Johnson

ASIAN NOODLE SALAD
28 Springs

This oversized eatery in downtown Siloam Springs is the brainchild of Shelley and Todd Simmons, who wanted to bring modern upscale dining to the downtown area. Opened in 2012, this sprawling restaurant features new fusion fare showcasing local ideas with innovative combinations. The blue corn muffins served with a housemade raspberry jam are a particular delight, as is the selection of bar-made sodas. It's this hickory grilled steak with Asian slaw, peanuts, mango, rice noodles, cilantro, arugula and ginger-soy dressing, that encapsulates the well-coordinated flavors served in this space.

100 East University Street * Siloam Springs
(479) 524-2828 * 28springs.com

9

ROAST DUCK and THE BAVARIAN PLATE
The Bavarian Inn Restaurant

German country foods are served in this comfortable chalet-style eatery that has graced Eureka Springs for generations. Succulent roasted duck with Bohemian-style dumplings, the perfectly roasted pork loin and crispy potato pancakes of the Bavarian plate, even the luscious and sought-after apple dumpling are all reasons to come back again.

325 West Van Buren (US Highway 62), Eureka Springs
(479) 253-8128 * Restaurant.EurekaSpringsInn.com

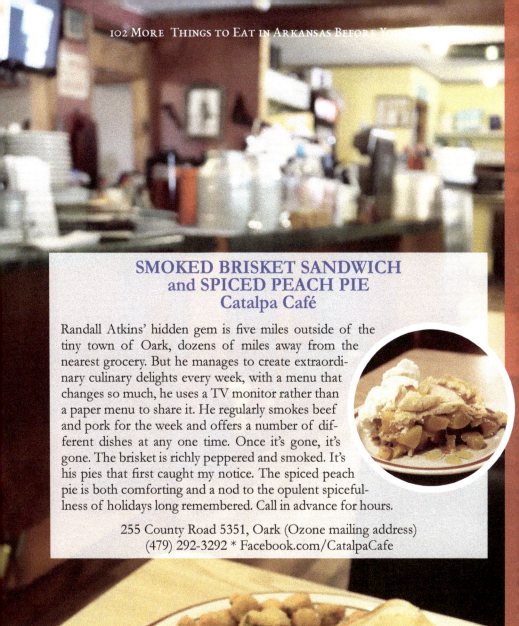

SMOKED BRISKET SANDWICH and SPICED PEACH PIE
Catalpa Café

Randall Atkins' hidden gem is five miles outside of the tiny town of Oark, dozens of miles away from the nearest grocery. But he manages to create extraordinary culinary delights every week, with a menu that changes so much, he uses a TV monitor rather than a paper menu to share it. He regularly smokes beef and pork for the week and offers a number of different dishes at any one time. Once it's gone, it's gone. The brisket is richly peppered and smoked. It's his pies that first caught my notice. The spiced peach pie is both comforting and a nod to the opulent spicefullness of holidays long remembered. Call in advance for hours.

255 County Road 5351, Oark (Ozone mailing address)
(479) 292-3292 * Facebook.com/CatalpaCafe

11

CHEESEBURGER AND FRIES
CJ's Butcher Boy Burgers

Richard Wilson's dream of a burger stand began in the old Waffle House in Russellville back in 2005. Its menu is extraordinarily simple - burgers, fries, shakes, sodas - and today it sticks to the quartet. The concentration on just a few items shows in the quality of perfectly smashed burgers that start out as chuck shoulders ground on-site and the consistency of potatoes that are cut when you order your meal. Bacon, mushrooms, grilled onions, jalapeños and a couple of choices in cheese are the only add-ons you need.

2803 North Arkansas Avenue, Russellville * (479) 968-2300
3484 West Wedington Drive, Fayetteville * (479) 249-9989
ButcherBoyBurger.com

SWEET AND SAVORY CRÊPES
Crêpes Paulette

Bentonville native Paula Jo Chitty Henry and her French husband Frédéric Henry began serving buckwheat crêpes from their food truck in 2010 and became an instant hit. Today the eatery's two locations both offer a significant selection of sweet and savory handhelds, which come out in reusable cups for easy serving. Try the KUAF, filled with Feta, pesto, tomatoes and either chicken or baby spinach, named for a local public radio station. Go savory with La Reubenesque, a turkey Reuben in a crêpe, or a sweet treat like the strawberry cheesecake or Nutella filled varieties.

213 Northeast A Street (food truck), Bentonville
100 Southwest 8th Street, Suite 4 (Storefront), Bentonville
(479) 250-1110 * CrepesPaulette.com

13

THE MOUNTAINBURGER
Dairy Dream

Arkansas's only loose-meat burger, this is a combination of ground beef, onions and spices served on a seedless bun with the suggestion of mustard and onion to create a unique soft sandwich experience. Get it along with a purple cow or silver saddle at this longstanding Boston Mountain Scenic Byway dairy bar - but only in season; the Dairy Dream closes in the off-season.

1600 US Highway 71, Mountainburg
(479) 369-2295

SHROOM SWISSALAKA
Feltner Brothers

Three of the grandsons of Bob Feltner, the man who originally opened Feltner's Whatta-Burger in Russellville in 1967, now have their own burger joint that celebrates the excellent flavor of those old burgers with new, thoughtful twists. Enter the Shroom Swissalaka, a mushroom cheeseburger that combines Swiss cheese, Dad's Mushrooms (seasoned and grilled) and Feltner's special sauce for a super savory sensation. The hot dogs are also sublime.

2768 North College Avenue, Fayetteville * (479) 935-4545
992 East Henri De Tonti Boulevard, Springdale * (479) 365-2907
FeltnerBrothers.com

PIES
Fork and Crust

Lori Rae's pie shop never had a chance to be little; the Rogers location took off so quick the store could barely keep up with orders. Considering the combinations of high-quality ingredients and the attention to detail by the staff, it's no wonder. Today, Fork and Crust's original location is always buzzing, as is the darling Fayetteville house that shares the name and the business. Seasonal pies such as this blackberry-peach slice are sought after, as are the standards such as cherry crumb and raspberry chiffon.

5208 West Village Parkway #11, Rogers * (479) 268-6634
600 North Mission Boulevard, Fayetteville * (479) 445-6925
ForkAndCrust.com

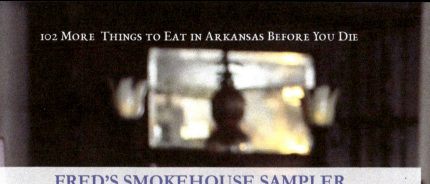

FRED'S SMOKEHOUSE SAMPLER
Fred's Hickory Inn

Tender pork loin, smoked sirloin and andouille sausage are sliced thin and served with a homemade barbecue sauce, a fitting spread for the eatery that Sam Walton called his favorite. The smoked sirloin that became famous as a prime rib served smoked rather than grilled shines best in this application.

1502 North Walton Boulevard, Bentonville
(479) 273-3303 * FredsHickoryInn.co

17

PAD SEE-EW
Fried Rice

A dish of flat rice noodles sautéed in a savory sauce with beef, chicken or shrimp, along with egg, broccoli and carrot for a gigantic dish that easily feeds two - at a restaurant where everything is under $10. The combination fried rice, spring rolls and Pad Thai also rank amongst the best in the state.

3758 Midland Boulevard, Fort Smith * (479) 783-7500
3802 Towson Avenue, Fort Smith * (479) 226-3946

BRISKET MELT
The Grapevine Restaurant

Open since 1991 in the old 22 Café location, this family-run operation focuses on homemade experiences, in particular a fantastic fresh baked white bread it slices for its sandwiches and to serve every diner with butter and honey. The Brisket Melt pairs that bread with house smoked brisket and homemade barbecue sauce, plus cheddar cheese, for a hearty, unforgettable sandwich.

105 East Walnut Street, Paris
(479) 963-2413
TheGrapevineRestaurant.com

THE TRULY GRAND STEAK
The Grand Taverne

A massive, 48 ounce Tomahawk of beef expertly roasted and served (appropriately enough) on a cutting board makes an impressive entrée to be shared. Chef Jeff Clements' diminutive kitchen sprouts lavish dishes of the finest delicacies, from pan seared scallops in lobster butter sauce to fried green tomatoes layered with pimento cheese and served with a dollop of bacon jam. Not on the menu - foie gras, one of the few places you'll find the rare item on any Arkansas menu.

37 North Main Street, Eureka Springs
(479) 253-6756 * EurekaGrand.com

FILET MIGNON or GRILLED PORK CHOP
Grotto Wood-Fired Grill and Wine Cave

Nestled below Spring Street along an exposed cave wall, this hole-in-the-wall location belies a splendid cavern of dining delights, where elegant foods come cleanly to be showcased on the table. Perfectly rare aged Creekmore beef melts in your mouth. Grotto eschews traditional side dishes in favor of smoked corn medleys, divinely roasted acorn squash and wine-soaked tenderly grilled mushrooms. Try the marrow.

10 Center Street, Eureka Springs
(479) 363-6431 * GrottoEureka.com

ARKANSAS FOOD HALL of FAME
WINNER

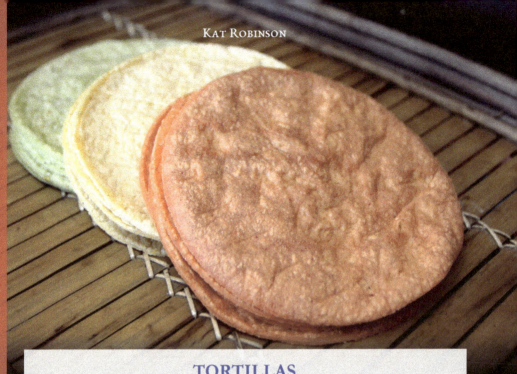

TORTILLAS
Mamma Z's Tortilla And Tamale Factory

Organic corn - white, yellow and blue - processed through nixtamalization, ground and blended with water and salt to create these honest, clean and bright tortillas. The color comes from the corn and from natural additives: peppers for red, spinach and kale for green, and beets for purple. Rosalba Zapata's fine creations are also available as tortilla chips and served alongside dishes in more than a dozen northwest Arkansas restaurants.

2503 South Walton Boulevard Suite 11, Bentonville
(614) 886-4469 * MammaZ.business.site

LENGUA TACOS
Maria's Mexican Restaurant

This humble, reasonably priced Mexican eatery offers soft, sumptuous tamales, loaded burritos and a fine selection of tacos, included these amply stacked tacos of cilantro, white onion and tender cubed and roasted succulent beef tongue, almost barbacoa-soft and absolutely gratifying.

8640 Rogers Avenue, Fort Smith * (479) 452-2328
2813 West Walnut Street, Rogers * (479) 986-9276
2503 S Walton Boulevard, Bentonville * (479) 271-0920

DUCK TWO WAYS
Mockingbird Kitchen

Chef Chrissy Sanderson's veracious aviary-enhanced space showcases her generous talents in interpreting the Ozarks to the plate with noted creativity.. The luscious Duck Two Ways, a prime example, pairs roasted duck leg confit with sliced duck breast smoked with applewood, alongside smashed sweet potatoes, sautéed greens and a handcrafted molasses barbecue sauce. The creativity stems to dessert, where the state favorite possum pie is improved upon with top technique and ingredients to become the eatery's eponymous Mockingbird pie. Bring a friend to share this conversation space.

1466 North College Avenue, Fayetteville
(479) 435-6333 * MockingbirdKitchen.com

MUD MUFFIN
Mud Street Café

A meatless meal that appeals, this hot toasted English muffin comes topped with flat scrambled eggs, Cheddar cheese, sprouts, tomato, black olive, leaf lettuce and mayo, a complete handheld breakfast to brace you for a day of shopping and exploring on world famous Spring Street. Best with a hot cup of coffee.

22 South Main Street #G, Eureka Springs
(479) 253-6732
MudStreetCafe.com
also 28 South Main Street, Eureka Springs
(479) 253-5399
MudStreetAnnex.com

CHICKEN SCHNITZEL, BURRATA, GNOCCHI
The Preacher's Son

Who knew gluten-free could be this good? Chef Matt Cooper's diligence to keeping a clean space within the walls of a splendid old church in the heart of downtown Bentonville has lead to the creation of an ever-evolving menu of delights featuring local farm produce and meats, innovative re-imagining of comfort food dishes, and a veritable kaleidoscope of bursting color. An eye-opening experience. The carrot gnocchi is a personal favorite. And don't feel guilty with this schnitzel; it's just as hearty and substantially savory fritter as you'd every hoped for. You will leave satisfied.

201 Northwest A Street, Bentonville
(479) 445-6065 * ThePreachersSon.com

KEEMA SAMOSAS
R & R Curry Express

Fresh ground lamb paired with fresh ground spices and bits of caramelized onion, carefully folded and deep fried, served with fresh mint and tamarind sauces, makes for the perfect Indian snack at both of the locations for this homegrown curry house. Enough for lunch by themselves, lovely for sharing, these samosas are the start of a beautiful repast. Enjoy watching the Tandoori Cam while you wait.

1525 Rogers Avenue, Fort Smith * (479) 494-5520
RRsCurryExpress.com
2576 West Sunset Avenue #C, Springdale * (479) 717-6500
RRCurryExpress.com

27

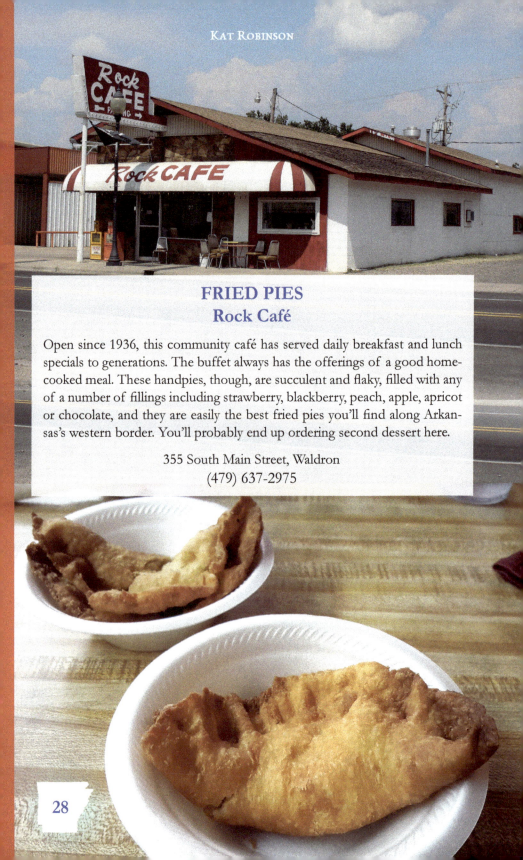

FRIED PIES
Rock Café

Open since 1936, this community café has served daily breakfast and lunch specials to generations. The buffet always has the offerings of a good home-cooked meal. These handpies, though, are succulent and flaky, filled with any of a number of fillings including strawberry, blackberry, peach, apple, apricot or chocolate, and they are easily the best fried pies you'll find along Arkansas's western border. You'll probably end up ordering second dessert here.

355 South Main Street, Waldron
(479) 637-2975

CHILI CHEESEBURGER
Sam's Olde Tyme Hamburgers

This mainstay of Rogers burger joints can be found by its giant Samasaurus hovering over the restaurant. Its burgers are equally monstrous, with the house seasoned third pound patties starring on a barbecue bacon burger, a blue cheese burger and even the Samasaurus with its jalapeños, pepper jack, Canadian bacon, American bacon, onions and Onion rings and Dino sauce. But to truly draw the attention of other diners, order up this chili-smothered sandwich and dig in with a fork... or spoon.

223 East Locust Street, Rogers
(479) 986-9191 * samshamburgers.com

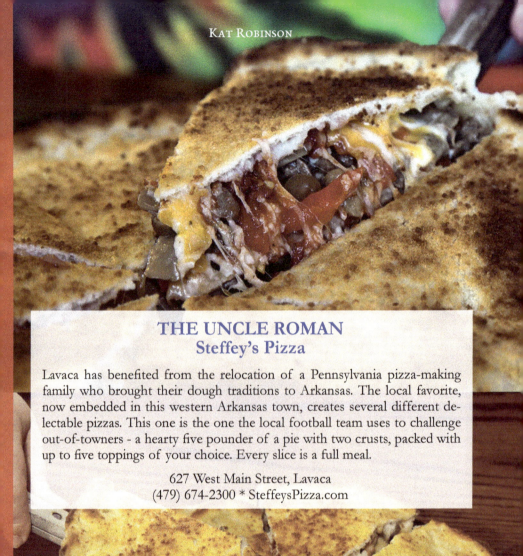

THE UNCLE ROMAN
Steffey's Pizza

Lavaca has benefited from the relocation of a Pennsylvania pizza-making family who brought their dough traditions to Arkansas. The local favorite, now embedded in this western Arkansas town, creates several different delectable pizzas. This one is the one the local football team uses to challenge out-of-towners - a hearty five pounder of a pie with two crusts, packed with up to five toppings of your choice. Every slice is a full meal.

627 West Main Street, Lavaca
(479) 674-2300 * SteffeysPizza.com

CHILI OMELET
Susan's Restaurant

Chili? In an omelet? You betcha. Susan's classic diner-style chili with beans, tomatoes, onions and bell peppers is the superb filling for the restaurant's expertly folded omelet, and a grand accompaniment to hash browns or hand-cut O'Brien potatoes on the side. Check out what's in the pie case while you're at it.

1440 West Sunset Avenue, Springdale
(479) 751-1445

SUSIE Q MALT SHOP

BURGERS AND MALTS
Susie Q's Malt Shop

Named for a piece of restaurant equipment, opened before the popular Creedence Clearwater Revival tune, this classic 50s style dairy bar retains the aesthetic of the era, down to the perfect malt and adorably composed drive in style burgers.

612 North Second Street, Rogers
(479) 631-6258

32

WHOLE DUCK
Tang's Asian Market

Shu Lan Tang followed in her parents' footsteps, opening this grocery alongside the main north-south artery through Springdale in 2013. Within, lunch specials of roasted duck, smoked pork belly and barbecue pork are paired with rice and seaweed salad. Order a whole or half duck, and receive it hot, steamy and sweet to take with you.

224 South Thompson Street, Springdale
(479) 751-1828 * Facebook.com/TangsAsianMarket

BUCKWHEAT PANCAKES
Bean Palace Restaurant at War Eagle Mill

One of the most famous sights in Arkansas is the three story mill rising alongside a wrought-iron bridge on the War Eagle River. Within, one can purchase any number of organic grain flours produced by the longstanding company. On its third floor, you'll find some of the best cornbread, muffins and pancakes, all created from these products. The buckwheat pancakes, served with maple syrup and butter, evoke memories of time gone by. If you cannot climb the stairs, place your order downstairs to go.

11045 War Eagle Road, Rogers
(866) 492-7324 * WarEagleMill.com

34

BRISKET
Wright's Barbecue

This book was held for a couple of weeks to allow me the chance to visit this Johnson establishment, thanks to dozens of individuals who insisted I must give it a try. My readers were right. This succulent, fall-apart brisket and its smoky bark are only surpassed by Wright's exuberantly peppery Thick & Sweet sauce. The Loaded Mac and Cheese is a sinful mouthful.

2212 Main Drive, Fayetteville
(Johnson community)
(479) 313-8618
WrightsBarbecue.com

NORTH CENTRAL

- [ ] 178 Club, Bull Shoals
- [ ] Big Spring Trading Company, St. Joe
- [ ] Blacksheep BBQ, Yellville
- [ ] Chow on the Square, Cherokee Village
- [ ] Daisy Queen, Marshall
- [ ] Elizabeth's Restaurant, Batesville ✗
- [ ] Fred's Fish House, Batesville/Mammoth Spring/ Mountain Home
- [ ] Jo Jo's Catfish Wharf, Mountain View
- [ ] Mona Lisa Café, Shirley
- [ ] Natalie's, Batesville
- [x] Nima's Pizza, Gassville w/ AOJ
- [ ] The Skillet Restaurant at the Ozark Folk Center, Mountain View
- [ ] Skipper's Restaurant, Mountain Home
- [ ] Skylark Café, Leslie
- [ ] Whispering Woods Grill and Cabin, Jordan
- [x] Who Dat's, Bald Knob w/ AOJ

GARLIC AND PARMESAN ENCRUSTED WALLEYE
178 Club

Bull Shoals' finest dining can be found in the dark paneled rooms of its famed 178 Club. But the same extraordinary, crispy walleye can be ordered in the attached bowling alley that's been part of the eatery's property for more than 30 years. Fried, blackened, grilled and broiled walleye also available.

2109 Central Boulevard, Bull Shoals
(870) 445-4949 * 178Club.com

RUNTS
Big Springs Trading Company

It's hard to choose just one dish from this Buffalo National River snack spot. The smoked meats and cheeses, the daily specials, the nachos and the desserts all shine. But if you just want to try everything all at once, you can't beat these quadruplet sandwiches: four sliders, each with one smoked meat - ham, roast beef, turkey and pork loin - topped with cheeses also smoked in-house. Served with barbecue sauce and a smile. Be sure to get some sliced smoked meat to go.

14237 North US Highway 65, St. Joe
(870) 439-2900 * BigSpringsRestaurant.com

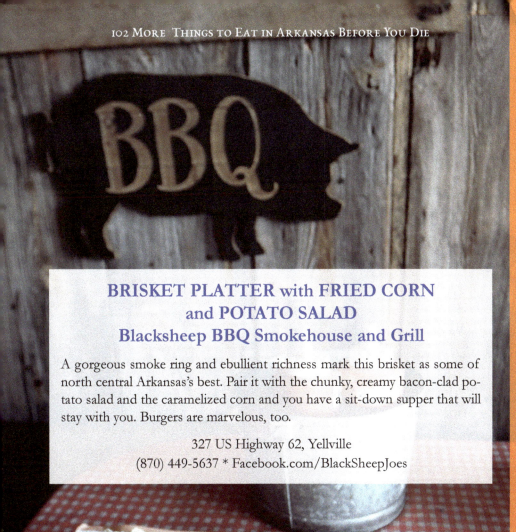

BRISKET PLATTER with FRIED CORN and POTATO SALAD
Blacksheep BBQ Smokehouse and Grill

A gorgeous smoke ring and ebullient richness mark this brisket as some of north central Arkansas's best. Pair it with the chunky, creamy bacon-clad potato salad and the caramelized corn and you have a sit-down supper that will stay with you. Burgers are marvelous, too.

327 US Highway 62, Yellville

(870) 449-5637 * Facebook.com/BlackSheepJoes

BLACK AND BLUE and PIMENTO CHEESE, BACON AND BLACKBERRY JAM SANDWICHES
Chow on the Square

The sister restaurant to Paragould's Chow at One Eighteen, this sunny spot in the Cherokee Village Town Center has become the community's get-and-go for good food. Chef Jeff Penn's menu changes seasonally, but his take on PB&J is a delectable winner. Get pie if he has a slice out when you go.

1 East Cherokee Village Mall #106, Cherokee Village
(870) 710-7047

BURGERS and ICE CREAM
Daisy Queen

The largest menu offered in all of Searcy County, Daisy Queen is always a crowd-pleaser. Since its opening in 1966, it has charmed generations of locals and lured passing tourists off the road for an old fashioned dairy bar experience complete with hot dogs, burgers, catfish, chicken sandwiches, Tex-Mex, fries, and so many other good eats. Every time a new dish receives good notice, it goes on one of the many menu boards. Take a few minutes off your trip up US Highway 65 to enjoy a shake and a burger.

614 US Highway 65, Marshall
(870) 448-2180 * Facebook.com/DaisyQueen1966

41

SALAD SAMPLER
Elizabeth's Restaurant

Fruit salad, green salad and a scoop of Elizabeth's delectable chicken salad comprise this light but delightful repast at the downtown Batesville lunchroom. The house dressing is exceptional, as are the fluffy rolls served with honey butter.

CLOSED?

231 East Main Street, Batesville
(870) 698-0903

CATFISH DINNER
Fred's Fish House

Dating back to 1991, Fred Ward's concept of fresh fish pulled right out of an Arkansas pond and served in the custom of our state with green tomato relish, coleslaw, beans and hush puppies continues to flourish in three locations in north central Arkansas. The Batesville location, housed in a former church, has made a family table of the baptistry and brought an enlightening and delightful meal experience to the parishioners of this fine fish house.

3777 Harrison Street, Batesville * (870) 793-2022
44 Arkansas Highway 101 Cutoff, Mountain Home * (870) 492-5958
215 Main Street, Mammoth Spring * (870) 625-7551
FredsFishHouse.com

43

GRILLED CATFISH
JoJo's Catfish Wharf

The Arkansas catfish feast comes to table here alongside gorgeous views of the White River at Jack's Resort above Mountain View. The delightfully savory unbreaded catfish fingers come speckled with house spice and are served with lemon for an extra piquant kick. Ample amounts of hush puppies, brown beans, coleslaw and green tomato relish accompany. Save room for possum pie.

237 Jacks Resort Road, Mountain View
(870) 585-2121 * JacksResort.com

44

WHATEVER LISA WANTS TO SERVE YOU
Mona Lisa Café

There's no cell signal in the little community of Shirley, no stoplight and no one telling you that you must pull into this quaint little restaurant that looks like someone's home. But you should, whenever you're hungry and the door is open.

Lisa has menus for breakfast and lunch but it's whatever she decides she wants to cook each day in her kitchen that you need to order - whether it's a daily lunch special, a casserole or some waffles served with butter-laden molten syrup. Call ahead to see if there's a buffet offered that particular day.

500 Arkansas Highway 9, Shirley
(501) 723-4848

CHICKEN SPAGHETTI
Natalie's

The Cajun runs strong in this Batesville lunchroom full of lavish color, New Orleans decor and scrumptious dishes. Natalie's is well known not only for paninis, avocado egg salad and an open faced pork pot roast sandwich, but for the heart-warming casseroles you can take home and for the delicate and delightful catering foods that grace so many area wedding receptions and parties. Natalie's version of the Arkansas cold weather staple chicken spaghetti comes with a rich base and thin noodles and a side, such as the too-good-to-pass-up spinach artichoke dip. Look for pie tarts and an exceptional pumpkin roll in the cold case.

3050 Harrison Street, Batesville
(870) 698-0200 * WhoDatNats.com

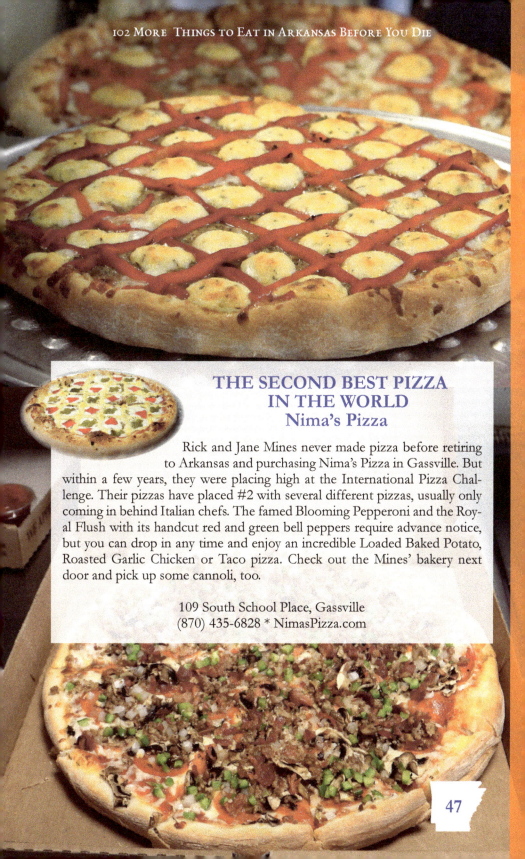

THE SECOND BEST PIZZA IN THE WORLD
Nima's Pizza

Rick and Jane Mines never made pizza before retiring to Arkansas and purchasing Nima's Pizza in Gassville. But within a few years, they were placing high at the International Pizza Challenge. Their pizzas have placed #2 with several different pizzas, usually only coming in behind Italian chefs. The famed Blooming Pepperoni and the Royal Flush with its handcut red and green bell peppers require advance notice, but you can drop in any time and enjoy an incredible Loaded Baked Potato, Roasted Garlic Chicken or Taco pizza. Check out the Mines' bakery next door and pick up some cannoli, too.

109 South School Place, Gassville
(870) 435-6828 * NimasPizza.com

47

OZARK SAMPLER PLATE
Skillet Restaurant at the Ozark Folk Center

A hearty, beloved selection of Arkansas favorites, this platter of greens, beans with ham, chicken and dumplings, fried okra and cornbread is an encapsulated expression of just how good Ozark country foods can be, a very definition to the term "stick-to-your-ribs." The fried chicken is also superlative. Get a window near the window to watch the squirrels and other wildlife outside.

1032 Park Avenue, Mountain View (at the Ozark Folk Center State Park)
(800) 264-3655

COUNTRY HAM AND EGGS BREAKFAST
Skipper's Restaurant

Long beloved in Mountain Home for its steaks and seafood, Skipper's also offers one of the best breakfast offerings in north central Arkansas, with ample portions and variety, from fajita omelets to country fried steak. This hefty slab of country ham is paired with eggs and your choice of biscuits and gravy or potatoes and toast is the perfect breakfast before getting out on the lake or off to work.

711 Arkansas Highway Five, Mountain Home
(870) 508-4574 * SkippersGoodFood.com

49

GREEN CHILE or VERDE SMOKED BRISKET TACOS
Skylark Café

Austin meets the Ozarks at this adorable café in a pretty little house in the tiny Leslie community. Here, there's always a pie on the counter, an expected delight for any country diner. But there are also southwestern favorites, from a verde tomatillo salsa to a variety of flour tortilla tacos, filled with smoked pork, beef or chicken. Sandwiches and salads also shine here.

401 High Street, Leslie
(870) 447-2354 * Facebook.com/SkylarkCafeLeslie

PARMESAN CRUSTED COD STIX
Whispering Woods Grill and Cabins

The charming resort not far from Norfork Dam offers high-end dining reasonably priced with steaks, seafood, pasta and pies all celebrated. Even amongst the considerable offerings, these "stix" are arguably the best fish sticks you'll ever enjoy in your life. Get a slice of Banofee pie while you're at it.

4245 Arkansas Highway 177, Jordan
(870) 499-5531 * WhisperingWoodsAR.com

FOOD BAR
Who Dat's

It's common to meet people from all over Arkansas dining at this Cajun restaurant in Bald Knob; the establishment is run by the Stelly family, formerly of Abbieville, Louisiana. This authentic taste of the bayou brings people in for red beans and rice, gumbo and the best Cajun food in the region. But it's the ample food bar, an add-on to any meal or a meal in itself, that's a true delight, with gravy steaks, spaghetti and meat sauce, potato stew, chicken tenders, corn on the cob, sweet yams and red beans and rice that keeps drawing folks back in.

3209 Arkansas Highway 367
North, Bald Knob
(501) 724-6183

NORTHEAST

- ☐ Al's BBQ, Trumann
- ☐ Dog N' Suds, Paragould
- ☐ Hamburger Station, Paragould
- ☐ Hen House Café, Piggott
- ☐ Jeri-Lin's Donuts, Blytheville
- ☐ Jerry's Steakhouse, Trumann
- ☐ JTown Grill, Jonesboro
- ☐ Kelley's Kickin' Chicken, West Memphis
- ☐ Kream Kastle, Blytheville
- ☐ Mike's Restaurant, Colt
- ☑ Ray's World Famous Bar-B-Que, West Memphis
- ☐ Sandbar Grille, Osceola
- ☐ Skinny J's, Paragould/Jonesboro/North Little Rock/Conway

CHICKEN TENDERS
Al's BBQ

This classic along Trumann's main drag has recently changed hands, but the legendary chicken strips that have gained the spot its fame since it first opened in 1972 remain unchanged. Succulent chicken battered with a light but savory breading make for an irresistible meal. Go for lunch buffets, where you can have as many chicken fingers as your heart desires.

229 Arkansas Highway 463, Trumann
(870) 483-6398

PUPUSAS and ROOT BEER
Dog N Suds

The southernmost location remaining of the once grand Dog N Suds chain is on the east side of Paragould. Today in addition to burgers, fries and the creamiest root beer, you'll find a selection of pupusas, ranging from bean and cheese to lorocco. Moving into the fusion realm has kept this location alive; but you'll still find it hard to beat one of the drive in's root beer floats.

319 East Kingshighway, Paragould
(870) 236-8511

HUMBURGER
Hamburger Station

All hail the Humburger, a big hand patted patty with plenty of black pepper, grilled in a pile of sliced onions, served with mustard and crunchy Kosher pickle chips on a toasted bun. It's the hallmark of Hamburger Station, a burger joint operating out of an old gas station by the tracks since 1985 and a favorite of Region 8. Outside dining only.

110 East Main Street, Paragould
(870) 239-9956 * Facebook.com/HamburgerStation

BLACKBOARD SPECIAL
Hen House Café

Need a good home-cooked meal? Every day, the folks at the Hen House Café on the square in downtown Piggott find something that'll warm your heart and cheer up your blues, whether it's pork chops, chicken and dumplings or pot roast on toast. This country-meets-city store-front makes sure you have good vittles to eat, and follows it up with marvelous pies and cakes.

260 West Court Street, Piggott
(870) 634-6578 * Facebook.com/HenHouseCafe13

CARAMEL DOUGHNUTS and CINNAMON ROLLS
Jeri-Lin Donuts

Jerry and Linda Musser opened the original Blytheville doughnut shop back in 1969, and became the hot spot in town for local high school students to hang out. A few years ago, the shop moved to the recently closed local bowling alley and continued a tradition. Today, Melissa Grant is in charge of making sure each and every caramel glazed, fruit filled doughnut and cinnamon bun are absolute recreations of the proprietary flavor. Regulars will tell you to place that doughnut and that cinnamon roll together for the joy thy call "the Smush"

840 North 10th Street, Blytheville
(870) 763-9679

RIBEYE STEAK
Jerry's Steakhouse

Don't let the dive bar aesthetic fool you. Jerry's has some of the best steaks you'll find in the Upper Delta. Charbroiled steaks - ribeyes, sirloins and filet mignon - come to the table with a baked potato, Texas toast, slice of tomato and a pile of jalapeño slices. The restaurant grew its fame from its 1981 opening thanks to Jerry Pillow's modified Sears brand charcoal grill, over which he expertly tamed steaks, burgers and chicken. The best time to go is Thursdays, when Jerry's offers its Sweetheart Specials - a two-for-one deal with a large and small sirloin or large and small ribeye sold together for you and your sweetheart - or, you know, just for you. Try the mushrooms.

424 Arkansas Highway 463, Trumann
(870) 483-1649 * JerrysSteakhouse.com

59

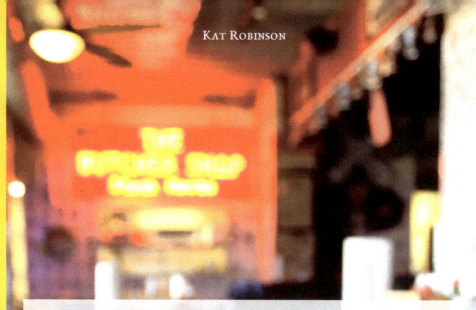

ELVIS PANCAKES
JTown's Grill

This hangout across from Arkansas State University lets its audacious nature show (Gas Station Corn Nuggets, anyone?) with a span of different crazy nacho plates, Sloppy Joe sweet potato fries, smoked chicken dip, a Southern Pride sandwich with pimento cheese, fried green tomatoes and bacon slaw, and crazy hot dogs, tacos and burgers. But it's this overachiever of a breakfast plate featuring chocolate and peanut butter chip pancakes sandwiching more peanut butter and slices of bacon, that really showcases just how far this restaurant staff will go to satisfy the cravings of hungry college students.

2610 East Johnson Avenue, Jonesboro
(870) 275-6514 * JTownsGrill.com

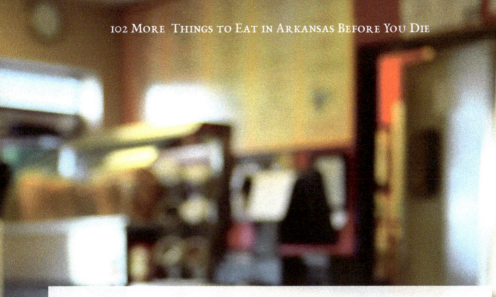

HONEYGOLD WINGS
Kelley's Kickin' Chicken

More than a dozen flavors, from naked to spicy hot to jerk, buffalo, barbecue and garlic are on the menu at this drive-thru, which also offers everything from Philly cheesesteaks to pork skins, turnip greens and hot dogs. These saucy, sweet and tangy Honeygold wings may be Arkansas's best chicken wings. Get a side of the salty, biting fried banana peppers, too. Expect a wait.

1397 North Missouri Street, West Memphis
(870) 400-0013

61

PIG SANDWICH
Kream Kastle

Simple, humble smoked pork butt on a seedless bun with a thin barbecue sauce and shredded coleslaw. It's the star on the menu at this old school drive-in eatery, held up as one of the paragons of Blytheville's famed barbecue scene. Open since 1953.

112 North Division Street, Blytheville
(870) 762-2366

ARKANSAS FOOD HALL of FAME
FINALIST

STEAK DINNER
Mike's Family Restaurant

Crowley's Ridge inhabitants from Jonesboro to Forrest City know great family celebrations happen at Mike's. A fine selection of dishes are always available, including catfish and shrimp. This ample steak dinner comes with dinner salad and choice of potato, and is rather popular. Check out the daily pie special.

49 Old Military Road West, Colt
(870) 633-8916

Joey N. Good eating

BARBECUE CHICKEN and RIBS
Ray's World Famous B-B-Q

2/28/2025 w/ sonjee ♡

Ray Gage's garden shed is home to his direct smoke pit, where pork and beef ribs and whole chickens are caressed by hickory smoke for hours on end. Ray himself keeps the CB on, and goes out to meet truckers who call on channel 16 with their orders. The pit gives the meat a grand flavor; folks who drop in also tend to go home with a slice of cake off the counter.

1805 N Missouri St. West Memphis

~~4114 East Service Road, West Memphis~~

(870) 732-2044

CATFISH PLATE
Sandbar Grille

Well known for its steaks, Harry Keatts' restaurant lures in plenty of folks for its crispy fried catfish and sweetly savory hush puppies. Its pies are also well known across Mississippi County. Go on a weeknight - the Grille is closed on Saturday and Sunday.

1100 West Keiser Avenue, Osceola
(870) 563-5700

65

REUBEN EGGROLLS
Skinny J's

The first of this expanding selection of restaurants began in 2009 in Paragould. The comfortable, laid-back bar and steakhouse operation offers some outrageous dishes, such as the Juicy J - a hot mess piled on a pepper Jack grilled cheese sandwich with a burger patty, topped with chicken, cheese dip, mushrooms, peppers, onions and tomatoes. There are also bacon confit wings tossed in a choice of seasonings, pimento cheese chicken with fried jalapeños, and these marvelous corned beef and kraut eggrolls with a Russian dressing dip. Great selection of beer on tap, too.

117 North Pruett Street, Paragould *(870)236-2390
205 South Main Street, Jonesboro * (870)275-6264
314 North Main Street, North Little Rock * (501)916-2645
2235 Dave Ward Drive, Conway * (501)358-6586
SkinnyJs.com

SOUTHEAST

- [ ] Beech Street Bistro, Crossett
- [ ] Country Kitchen, Pine Bluff
- [ ] Fox's Pizza Den/Cowboy's Steaks, Lake Village
- [ ] Hurley House Café, Hazen
- [ ] Lybrand's Bakery, Pine Bluff
- [ ] Mammoth Orange Café, Redfield
- [ ] Pine Bluff Country Club, Pine Bluff
- [ ] Southbound Tavern, Helena-West Helena
- [ ] Troy's Drive-In, DeWitt

FRIED CRAWFISH AND SHRIMP
Beech Street Bistro

Tucked into a neighborhood off the main drive through Crossett, Chester and Laura Huntsman's renovated shotgun shack is the hot spot for good eating in the Lower Arkansas town. The rhythm and blues aesthetic tie together Cajun and Creole fare with country cooking, with prime crispy crawfish and shrimp a star to hang an eatery on. The country fried steak may be the best you can get along the south Arkansas border. Stick around, and Chester might pull out one of his many musical instruments for a personal concert. Feel free to sing along.

202 Beech Street, Crossett
(870) 304-2183
BeechStreetBistro.com

CHILI CHEESEBURGER
Country Kitchen

Homemade chili made from scratch each day and hand patted well sea-soned beef patties combine to make the best chili cheeseburger you'll find in the state at this classic country diner that's sat on Dollarway Road since it opened in 1953. The restaurant is well known for country breakfasts and an ever-changing plate lunch special that often includes a choice of fried or smothered pork chops, fried chicken, chicken and dress-ing, hamburger steak, pepper steak, meatloaf or catfish with so many sides to choose from - steamed cabbage, baked beans, green beans, fried okra and deviled eggs among them. Stay for a slice of housemade lemon icebox pie.

4322 Dollarway Road, White Hall
(870) 535-4767
CountryKitchenAndBanquetBarn.com

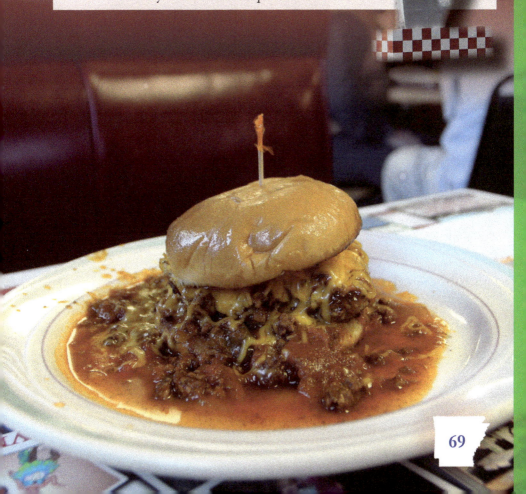

SMALL STEAK
Cowboy's Steaks within Fox's Pizza Den

A restaurant within a restaurant? That's what you get in Lake Village, where Santa Lee offers his prime ribeyes and strips inside the Fox's Pizza Den location he runs with his family. The restaurant, already known for baking the largest pizza in Arkansas (a 30" pie!), serves pizzas, subs, "wedgie" sandwiches and salads. Add in the magnificent handcut steaks served with tiny potatoes and you have one of the most surprising dining locations in the Lower Delta. The small steak is ample; the large is enough for two. Cooked to order; expect a wait.

1927 US Highway 65, Lake Village
(870) 265-3691

HOT CHILI
Hurley House Café

This stop-for-a-bite café along US Highway 70 serves country favorites in a laid back setting - with breakfasts, catfish, a nice variety of sandwiches and plated dinners. It's also popular for its country vittle lunch buffet. But the meat-heavy, rich chili is worth the stop, the perfect bowl of nourishment to warm you back up after a morning of duck hunting. Fried pies are always available.

92 South Maple Street, Hazen
(870) 255-4679

71

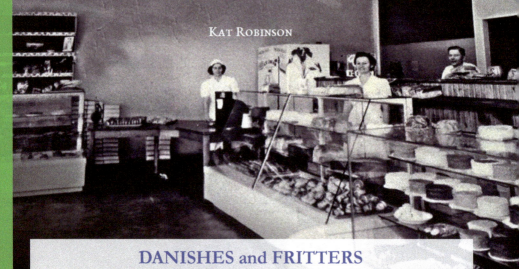

DANISHES and FRITTERS
Lybrand's Bakery

This family operation began in downtown Pine Bluff in 1940. It's well known for providing cakes for a large portion of southeast Arkansas's weddings, and serves a mean quiche. Doughnuts are airy, and the fritters, available in various flavors by day including blueberry, cherry and apple, are substantially filling. The danishes, like this blueberry version, are delightful.

2900 South Hazel Street, Pine Bluff
(870) 534-4607 * Facebook.com/LybrandsBakery

SUNDAES
Mammoth Orange Café

Designed after the round orange dairy bars originally created by Frank E. Pohl in 1926 in California. Ernestine Bradshaw opened this Arkansas edition in the Redfield community in the 1960s. Today, the operation is run by her grandson, Jock Carter, who has kept the menu much the same. Burgers and ice cream delights dot the menu, and it's worth your time to dine in and enjoy a sundae or milkshake in an ice cold glass.

103 Arkansas 365 North, Redfield
(501) 397-2347

73

PIMENTO CHEESE SKILLET
with TOMATO JAM and RAISIN BREAD
Pine Bluff Country Club

Chef Jamie McAfee's 16 years at this high-end establishment, paired with his 42 years in the restaurant business, gives him a boldness to approaching Arkansas food with a twist. This hot dip brazenly pairs several flavors to achieve a tangy and immensely satisfying appetizer. The bitingly sharp spice in the Pow Pow, created with shrimp or chicken, is a nice counterpoint.

1100 West 46th Avenue, Pine Bluff
(870) 535-0132 * PineBluffCC.com

NORWEGIAN SALMON
Southbound Tavern

This blues-oriented Cherry Street dive does a lot of things to please the crowds who come to hear local artists play on its stage. Its selection of burgers and flatbread pizzas is ample; its full-on dinners, such as this beautifully presented dish of salmon with avocado, wild rice and vegetables, gives downtown Helena visitors and locals a refreshing upscale experience in downhome digs.

233 Cherry Street, Helena-West Helena
(870) 228-5009 * SouthboundTavern.com

75

A BURGER and a CARAMEL SHAKE
Troy's Drive In

The classic dairy bar in DeWitt offers banana splits, barbecue and what it calls a Mex Pie (a Frito chili pie by another name). Its flamekist burgers bring back the memories of a time when the best burgers were always consumed at a picnic table or in a car after visiting such an establishment. Malts and shakes are on point.

1024 South Jefferson Street, DeWitt
(870) 946-1201

SOUTHWEST

- [ ] Bones Chophouse, Hot Springs/Little Rock
- [ ] Capo's Tacos, Hot Springs
- [ ] FayRay's, El Dorado
- [ ] Fish Bowl, Ashdown
- [ ] Magnolia Bake Shop, Magnolia
- [ ] Mr. Whiskers, Hot Springs
- [ ] Rocky's Corner, Hot Springs
- [ ] Shangri-La Resort, Mt. Ida
- [ ] Sue and Carol's Restaurant, Texarkana
- [ ] Suzy Q's Sweet Creams and Coffee, Mena
- [ ] Taco Mama, Hot Springs
- [ ] Tailgater's Burger Company, Hope
- [ ] The Backyard Barbecue Company, Magnolia
- [ ] Three Chicks Feed and Seed, Texarkana
- [ ] The Whippet Family Restaurant and Dairy Bar, Prattsville
- [ ] Williams Tavern Restaurant at Historic Washington State Park, Washington

CRAWFISH CORNBREAD and BONE-IN RIBEYE
Bones Chophouse

Tender, seasoned aged steaks, fresh flown-in seafood, and all the delightful details well observed make this steakhouse a worthy destination for any celebration. Add in the state's largest bourbon collection, adorably delectable appetizers such as a tower of cornbread in a gorgeously lavish crawfish cream... oh golly..

3920 Central Avenue, Hot Springs * (501) 520-5900
27 Rahling Circle, Little Rock * (501) 821-5800
BonesChophouse.com

78

TACOS and GUACAMOLE
Capo's Tacos

The eatery's website points to Michoacán street tacos for inspiration, but it's clear tacos are their own inspiration here. Available in seventeen different variety, most are just $3 each (seafood tacos are half a buck more), which encourages sampling, swapping and sharing. Whether it's carnitas, barbacoa, fried chicken, poblano peppers or red snapper, Capo's has taken great care to match up fresh and complementary ingredients for memorable bites. The guac is fresh; ask for a basket of duros (whole wheat pinwheels) for trying the multiple available salsas.

200 Higdon Ferry Road, Hot Springs
(501) 623-8226 * CaposTacos.com

ORLEANS PASTA
Fayray's

LA (Louisiana) meets LA (Lower Arkansas) at this romantic escape on the El Dorado downtown square. A fine selection of beverages accompany Chef Michael Rice's rich Creole spiced sauces and seafood to create this inviting, irresistible pasta dish. It's one of many on the menu that showcase excellent steaks, catfish, and side dishes at the perfect date-night rendezvous point. Save room for Crème brûlée, bread pudding or bourbon chocolate pecan pie.

110 East Elm Street, El Dorado
(870) 863-4000 * FayRays.site

WHOLE FRIED CATFISH and SET-UP
Fish Bowl

A good old-fashioned Arkansas catfish feast served just off the shore of Millwood Lake since 1972. Every catfish dinner comes to table with coleslaw, beans, green tomato relish, hush puppies (in this case, cylindrical), butter, white onion and lemon. Catfish fillets and grilled catfish are available, but this is one of the few places you'll find where fried whole catfish is also an option. If you finish any of your set-up, the staff will happily bring you more. You can even get the set-up on its own, an all-you-can-eat feast, for $5. Steaks, chicken strips and burgers also available.

1409 Arkansas Highway 32, Ashdown
(870) 898-2993 * FishBowlMillwood.com

81

MAGNOLIA BAKE SHOP

ITALIAN CREAM CAKE
Magnolia Bake Shop

The oldest continuously operating bakery in Arkansas has been at it since 1928. Doughnuts are available every morning, and you can go in for a marvelous variety of cookies, cakes and pies every day. This simple but rich Italian cream cake isn't tall, but it is packed with moist coconut, pecans, cream cheese and heavy cream. Worth a lengthy drive.

103 North Jefferson, Magnolia
(870) 234-1304 * Facebook.com/MagnoliaArkansasBakery

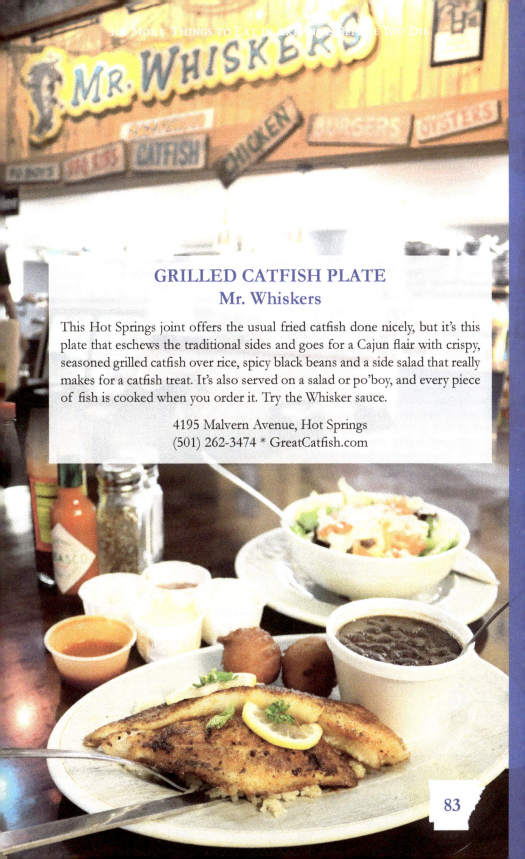

GRILLED CATFISH PLATE
Mr. Whiskers

This Hot Springs joint offers the usual fried catfish done nicely, but it's this plate that eschews the traditional sides and goes for a Cajun flair with crispy, seasoned grilled catfish over rice, spicy black beans and a side salad that really makes for a catfish treat. It's also served on a salad or po'boy, and every piece of fish is cooked when you order it. Try the Whisker sauce.

4195 Malvern Avenue, Hot Springs
(501) 262-3474 * GreatCatfish.com

83

KAT ROBINSON

PIZZA BIANCA
Rocky's Corner

The hottest spot across from Oaklawn Racing and Gaming is this Chicago-meets-the-Spa-City bar, which specializes in thick crust pizzas, bowls of pasta and a bevy of sandwiches. The Pizza Bianca, or White Pizza, shines best here when paired with house marinara for dipping. A great nightcap.

2600 Central Avenue, Hot Springs
(501) 624-0199

84

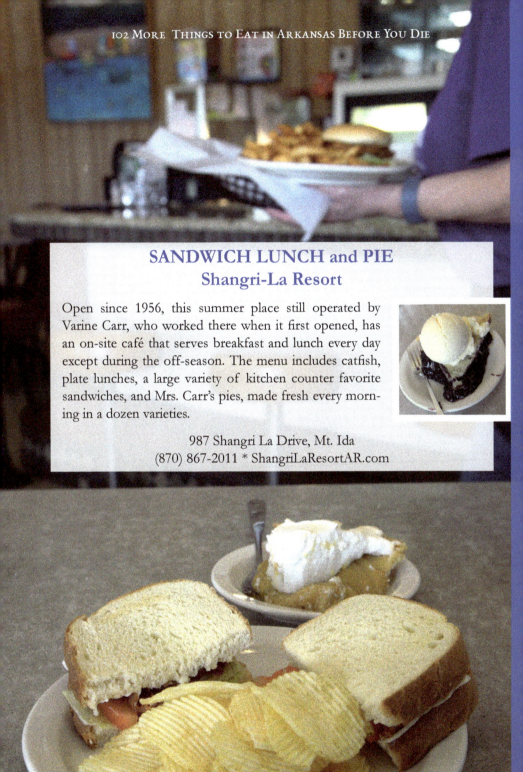

SANDWICH LUNCH and PIE
Shangri-La Resort

Open since 1956, this summer place still operated by Varine Carr, who worked there when it first opened, has an on-site café that serves breakfast and lunch every day except during the off-season. The menu includes catfish, plate lunches, a large variety of kitchen counter favorite sandwiches, and Mrs. Carr's pies, made fresh every morning in a dozen varieties.

987 Shangri La Drive, Mt. Ida
(870) 867-2011 * ShangriLaResortAR.com

85

PANCAKES and PIE
Sue and Carol's Kitchen

Opened in 1979 by Sue Sanders Hall and her daughter, Carol Rodenroth, this restaurant has always stood busy on quality breakfasts, comforting lunches and a nice selection of pie. The veal cutlet and chicken spaghetti are tops at lunch. At breakfast, pancakes are an excellent choice. But best of all, whether it's egg custard, strawberry cream, chocolate meringue or peach cream cheese, you can have a slice of pie with your bacon and eggs.

938 North State Line Avenue, Texarkana
(870) 774-0859

AFFOGATO
Suzie Q's Sweet Creams and Coffee

New to Mena's downtown strip, this adorable ice cream shop with a two story atrium offers soup and sandwiches alongside its sweet treats and coffee beverages. Go for an adult choice - a high octane espresso poured over a scoop of your favorite Yarnell's ice cream flavor. Best savored while relaxing on the porch swing hanging by its staircase.

601 Mena Street, Mena
(479) 216-6770 * Facebook.com/SuzyQs.Mena

GRILLED CORN QUESADILLAS
Taco Mama

Diane Bratton's restaurant, a working edifice that pays tribute to her mother, is treasured for its sincere efforts to utilize only fresh produce and meat and made from scratch tortillas, sauces and beverages to bring a true southwest flavor to the Spa City. Beautifully roasted peppers are always available to add to your dinner. These diminutive but flavor-packed foldover quesadillas come to the table packed with hot cotija cheese, cool guacamole and cold crema. Don't pass up the magnificent cilantro rice and black beans.

1209 Malvern Avenue, Hot Springs
(501) 624-6262 * TacoMama.net

GORGONZOLA BURGER
Tailgater's Burger Company

Want a lotta burger or a little burger? Tailgater's takes care of you. Combos are ordered by the patty size - a third of a pound or half a pound - and topped in a variety of ways, whether it's the Yankee with cheddar and barbecue sauce, the applewood bacon with provolone, or this version with a generous amount of Gorgonzola cheese applied directly to the hot patty, which melts the salty tangy topper right into the meat. Flywheel fried pies are on hand for dessert alongside ice cold milkshakes.

101 South Main Street, Hope
(870) 777-4444 * Facebook.com/TailgatersBurgerCompany

BARBECUE SANDWICH and PIE
The Backyard Barbecue Company

A sweet and smoky sauce works well to properly season the shredded beef and pork this eatery prepares for its devoted crowd. Tender ribs, beans packed with sausage, and a mighty selection of pies keep locals coming back.

1407 East Main Street, Magnolia
(870) 234-7890 * BackyardBarbecueCompany.com

CHICKEN SALAD SANDWICH
Three Chicks Feed, Seed and Café

Angie Watson, Dee Dee Rogers and Julie Miller bought into an old feed and seed store and took after it to create a fantastic farm life experience. Within a short time, the ladies had also taken in the Chuck Wagon, a small food truck, and incorporated it into the business. These days Julie is in charge of the café, creating a country diner in a quaint side space with mismatched tables, decades old memorabilia, and a menu that features eight burgers, six salads, and a wide array of sandwiches, including the hearty old-fashioned chicken salad, here served alongside long-cut mayo slaw. Lunch specials available daily.

4045 Genoa Road, Texarkana
(870) 773-5633 * ThreeChicksFeed.com

91

CATFISH
The Whippet Dairy Bar and Restaurant

The former Lovoie's Drive In, opened in 1966, received its permanent name in 1971 when it was purchased by the Holiman family. A few changeovers later, Derek and Debbie Henderson are now in charge, but you'd be hard pressed to find much if any changes in the past several decades. The catfish here is crispy and light. Burgers are ample, and each Tuesday night is steak night, with visitors coming in from several counties away.

9011 US Highway 270, Prattsville
(870) 699-4391 * TheWhippet.com

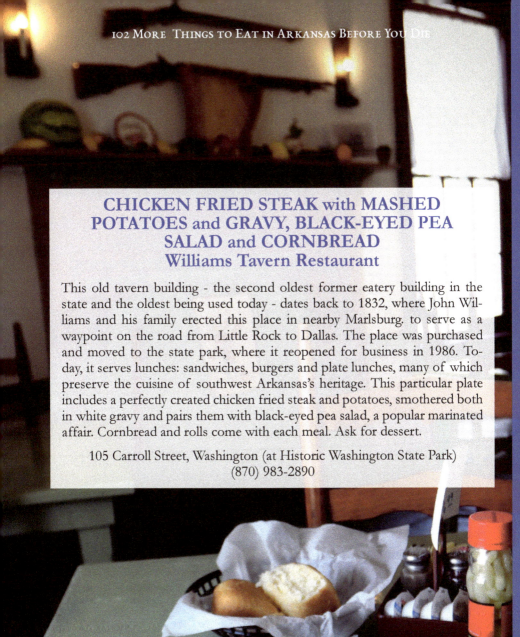

CHICKEN FRIED STEAK with MASHED POTATOES and GRAVY, BLACK-EYED PEA SALAD and CORNBREAD
Williams Tavern Restaurant

This old tavern building - the second oldest former eatery building in the state and the oldest being used today - dates back to 1832, where John Williams and his family erected this place in nearby Marlsburg. to serve as a waypoint on the road from Little Rock to Dallas. The place was purchased and moved to the state park, where it reopened for business in 1986. Today, it serves lunches: sandwiches, burgers and plate lunches, many of which preserve the cuisine of southwest Arkansas's heritage. This particular plate includes a perfectly created chicken fried steak and potatoes, smothered both in white gravy and pairs them with black-eyed pea salad, a popular marinated affair. Cornbread and rolls come with each meal. Ask for dessert.

105 Carroll Street, Washington (at Historic Washington State Park)
(870) 983-2890

93

CENTRAL

- [ ] A.W. Lin's, Little Rock
- [x] Big Orange, Little Rock
- [x] Boulevard Bread Company, Little Rock
- [ ] Brave New Restaurant, Little Rock
- [ ] Bruno's Little Italy, Little Rock
- [ ] Ciao Italian Restaurant, Little Rock
- [x] Dugan's Pub, Little Rock
- [ ] Gadwall's Grill, North Little Rock
- [ ] HB's Bar-B-Q, Little Rock
- [ ] Holly's Country Cookin', Conway
- [ ] Kemuri Sushi, Seafood, Robata, Little Rock
- [ ] Leo's Greek Castle, Little Rock
- [x] Loblolly Creamery, Little Rock
- [ ] One Eleven at the Capital, Little Rock
- [ ] Pea Farm Bistro, Cabot
- [ ] Red Door, Little Rock
- [ ] Salem Dairy Bar, Benton
- [ ] South on Main, Little Rock
- [ ] Taqueria Jalisco'z, Little Rock/North Little Rock
- [ ] Wagon Wheel Restaurant, Greenbrier
- [ ] WunderHaus, Conway

MALA BEEF SHANK CASSEROLE and KANI SU
A.W. Lin's

The depths of flavor in this hot pot go far beyond the braised and simmered beef chunks and bone. They combine a range of capsicum and peppercorns over a beef broth bursting with aspic and marrow, with carrot and mushroom and hints of ginger, star anise and clove that offset garlic notes. The hearty dish is a counterpoint to the delightfully light Kani Su, a salad of shredded crab and cucumber with Japanese mayo and crispy crunch. Together, these shared dishes are a harmonious feast.

17717 Chenal Parkway H-101 (Promenade on Chenal), Little Rock
(501) 821-5398 * AWLins.com

95

THAI CHOP SALAD
Big Orange

It takes a lot of guts to showcase salads alongside such a defining dish as burgers, but Big Orange has reason to be proud. This peanut-soy dressed greens and cabbage based salad clad in cilantro, basil and red pepper comes to the table with fresh chopped jalapeños, grape tomatoes and beautifully seared ribeye cooked to order. It's as beloved as any of the famed burgers on the menu or the Big Orange cheese dip, served with corn tortillas or, if you ask, the housemade Kennebec potato chips. Like the stop that sparked the inspiration for the name (Mammoth Orange Café in Redfield, see page 73), it blends milkshakes, though those offered here are both creative and bright in color.

17809 Chenal Parkway G-101, Little Rock * (501) 821-1515
207 North University Avenue #100, Little Rock * (501) 379-8715
2203 South Promenade Boulevard #3100, Rogers * (479) 202-5339
BigOrangeBurger.com

ARKANSAS FOOD HALL OF FAME
FINALIST

96

CHOCOLATE CROISSANT
Boulevard Bread Company

This bakery, where hand-crafted loaves have always starred, has expanded into soups, deli sandwiches, paninis and even brunch. But it's the simple, sweet morsels created each day that capture the heart - scones, macaroons, danishes and croissant that are best meant to accompany a coffee beverage and a conversation. The pliant, dark chocolate filled chocolate croissants are a measured quotient of joy to consume with a smudge of butter, a pastry that requires patience and reverence to fully enjoy. Best get two.

All in Little Rock:
1920 North Grant Street * (501)663-5951
1417 South Main Street * (501)375-5100
9601 Baptist Health Drive * (501) 217-4025
BoulevardBread.com

97

MIXED GRILL and MUSHROOM TART
Brave New Restaurant

Peter Brave is Little Rock's original mad culinary scientist, opening his eponymous eatery in 1991 and continuing to surprise and delight diners ever since. At lunchtime, his experiments have lead to a marvelous duck sausage served on Boulevard Bread bun; an eye-opening avocado and crabmeat salad with sections of grapefruit, and a sandwich made with Brave's own PurpleHull pea patty - itself a meatless wonder. At dinner, his dishes go full tilt - none expressing his abandon and glee more than the mixed grill of grilled pork tenderloin, a whole stuffed quail, wild game sausage and a beef medallion - a prodigious spread to satisfy any carnivore. Yet I am completely satisfied with his wild mushroom tart, with four or more different types of mushroom in cream and shallots, gorgeously caramelized. The restaurant's back deck offers one of the best views you can find of the Arkansas River in Little Rock.

ARKANSAS FOOD HALL of FAME
FINALIST

2300 Cottondale Lane #105, Little Rock
(501) 663-2677 * BraveNewRestaurant.com

LASAGNA IMBOTITO
Bruno's Little Italy

Jimmy Bruno is credited with bringing pizza to Arkansas back in 1949. Though the location has changed and the business has been handed down within the family, Bruno's Little Italy continues to serve fine Italian pastas, pizza and steaks. Its latest location, opened in 2013 in the heart of Main Street's burgeoning new Creative Corridor development, retains the warmth and history seven decades has wrought. With many fanciful dishes - Cream Scallops with Mushrooms, Fettuccine Shrimp Zucchini Pomodoro and the colossal Assorted Antipasto Ala Vincenzo come to mind - it is the ostentatious Lasagna Imbotito with its layers of Italian sausage, meatballs and cured meats between cheese, sauce and noodles that has received the most fame.

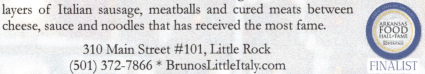

310 Main Street #101, Little Rock
(501) 372-7866 * BrunosLittleItaly.com

ARKANSAS
FOOD
HALL OF FAME
FINALIST

PESTO TORTELLINI, CRABCAKES and MUSHROOM BISQUE
Ciao Italian Restaurant

Like an old friend, Ciao is Little Rock's unpretentious Italian hole-in-the-wall, tucked back a block from Broadway on Seventh Street. With little advertising, visitors make it here on word-of-mouth and whispers of honest pastas and entrees. Dinners are intimate affairs, quiet and with plenty of atmosphere to enchant your date. Lunches are exceptionally priced, one of the best bargains you'll find downtown. The succulent crabcakes, with little filler, are a treat; the mushroom bisque an unctuous sigh of happiness. With a hot dish of pesto-clad tri-color cheese tortellini, you have a rewarding and comforting repast to remember fondly later. Half-sized desserts help keep those thoughts of guilt at bay.

405 West Seventh Street, Little Rock
(501) 372-0238 * CiaoItalianRestaurant.com

BUILD YOUR OWN BURGER
Dugan's Pub

Don Dugan's slice of the British Isles has become the hub of activity along Third Street downtown, earning its relaxed lunch crowd cred. This marvelous pub burger, cooked to order and with your choice of sides, cheese and vegetables, is juicy and satisfying. The Shepherd's Pie and the contents of the Dublin Coddle - pan seared Pacific cod and Irish bangers with caramelized onions and roasted potatoes in a bacon broth - are excellent accompaniments to a good stout.

401 East Third Street, Little Rock
(501) 244-0542 * DugansPubLR.com

CHICKEN NACHOS and WOMAN-MADE CHILI
Gadwall's Grill

This neighborhood bar and grill offers what you might expect from a friends-and-family joint - ample breakfasts, generous lunches and such. Gadwall's adds a layer of reliability and local interest to the concept, with chocolate gravy for morning biscuits, hand-shredded chicken and deep orange cheese dip for its nachos, and the hearty and bean-filled Woman Made chili for its burgers, chili dogs and just for enjoying with a basket of crackers.

7311 North Hills Boulevard #14, North Little Rock
(501) 834-1840 * GadwallsGrill.com

SLICED PORK OR BEEF PLATE
HB's Bar-B-Q

The heir to the celebrated The Shack BBQ, this tiny neighborhood hangout on Lancaster in southwest Little Rock retains its smoke, its full bodied sauce and its sweet-and-tangy potato salad, unchanged for decades. Sandwiches and plates come with white bread; for a change of pace, go for a Frito chili pie. Cash only.

6010 Lancaster Road, Little Rock
(501) 565-1930 * Facebook.com/HBsBarBQ

PLATE LUNCH SPECIAL
and BANANA CREAM PIE
Holly's Country Cookin'

Home cooking in its native form is offered cafeteria-style to patrons of this south Conway lunchroom. The meatloaf may be jagged, the macaroni and cheese less than picture perfect, but as is often said about such things around these parts, "it eats." Marvelously crusty fried chicken, gravy-smothered country fried steaks, ham-laden beans and fluffy rolls draw in regulars. Holly's banana cream pie is the best such example in the state.

120 Harkrider Street, Conway
(501) 328-9738 * HollysCountryCookin.com

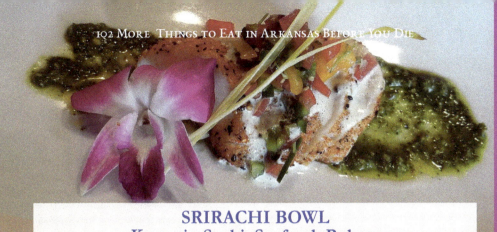

SRIRACHI BOWL
Kemuri - Sushi, Seafood, Robata

More than just a sushi restaurant, Kemuri shines as a destination where every care is given the dishes created within, for a modern Japanese aesthetic. Chef Alex Guzman's chromatic creativity at the sushi bar is matched with Chef Greg Wallis' intrigue with smoked meats and love of a hot coal grill. Together, the pair conjure thoughtful, edible masterpieces that elevate dining into art appreciation. The Sriracha Bowl is a mirthful creation with hand selected and cut fresh fish, masago, vegetables and flowers on a bed of roe-studded spicy rice, a well you'll keep dipping your chopsticks into with lust for each bite.

2601 Kavanaugh Boulevard, Little Rock
(501) 660-4100 * KemuriRestaurant.com

105

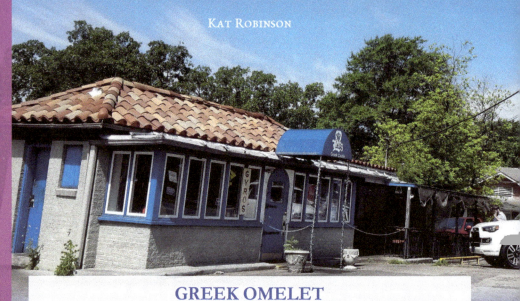

GREEK OMELET
Leo's Greek Castle

Housed in a building that's been a gas station and a barbecue joint in past lives, this little stop along Kavanaugh in Hillcrest is Little Rock's oldest gyro joint. Today, the four table dining room is plastered with hand-colored images of Leo the Lion. Gyros in many forms are highlighted on the menu. This creation, a breakfast favorite, packs the shaved lamb in with tomatoes, mushrooms, bell pepper and onion and cheddar cheese. Ask for it with Feta Best place around to get a cold PBR..

2925 Kavanaugh Boulevard, Little Rock
(501) 666-7414 * Facebook.com/LeosGreekCastle

ICE CREAMS OF ALL SORTS
Loblolly Creamery

4/27/2025
after
Hadestown

Sally Mengel's precious soda fountain shop and dreamy little ice cream truck both serve what you're craving - clean, locally sourced Arkansas flavors in varieties that change by the season. Whether it's a hefty scoop of Arkansas Mud, a Little Rock-Y Road, effervescent Honey Lavender or quirky Blueberry Cornbread, there's a flavor that will tempt you. Ask about ice cream flights.

1423 Main Street Suite C, Little Rock
(501) 503-5164 * LoblollyCreamery.com

EXPRESS LUNCH or PETIT DEJEUNER DE PARIS
One Eleven at the Capital

James Beard Award-winning Chef Joël Antunes has made the kitchen of the former Ashley's at the Capital his playground, injecting a little bit of Arkansas into regional French-inspired fare. Engage the Francophile in your life at breakfast with a spread of pastries, fruit and yogurt. If you can't spare the time for a leisurely dinner, carve out a slice of lunch and put yourself into Chef's hands with the Express Lunch; the combination of one of Joël's entrées alongside a soup, starter, cheese and dessert is a delightful way to experience his ingenuity.

111 West Markham Street, Little Rock
(501) 370-7011
CapitalHotel.com/One-Eleven

SMOKED TURKEY SANDWICH
with PICKLED ONIONS
Pea Farm Bistro

Andrea and Justin Wilson's popular Hot Rod Weiners food concession bloomed into this regardful sandwich shop in 2017. The eatery is number one with Cabotians looking for excellently prepared sandwiches on French rolls, Italian bread, rye or sourdough. Smoked turkey with avocado is high on the order list, especially with a little housemade pickled onion. So is the agreeable chicken salad with cranberries and pecans. Having a hard time deciding? Ask for a half and half with chicken salad and pimento cheese.

1102 South Pine Street, Suite 9, Cabot
(870) 210-6416 * Facebook.com/PeaFarmBistro

109

STUFFED MUSHROOMS and FRENCH COUNTRY SKILLET
Red Door

Chef Mark Abernathy's comfortably appointed house on the Rebsamen Park triangle is noted for being one of the best brunch locations in the state. If you're out and about in the morning, drop in for a gorgeous French Country Skillet, with Hollandaise over two eggs, asparagus, mushrooms and cheese, a sophisticated stack served with a fresh croissant. Or dig into the robust crab and lobster filled mushroom caps in a Tuscan veal sauce for a sturdy lunchtime spread.

3701 Cantrell Road, Little Rock
(501) 666-8482 * RedDoorRestaurant.net

BURGER AND FRIES
Salem Dairy Bar

It'd hard to get more old fashioned than this order-at-the-window dairy bar along Congo Road. Burgers come in regular and jumbo sizes with sides of crinkle fries. Ice cream is soft serve and best in sundaes or paired with a piping hot fudge fried pie.

6406 Congo Road, Benton * (501) 794-3929

111

HOPPIN' JOHN VEGGIE BURGER
South on Main

Created as a space to visualize the content and performance of writers and musicians featured in the Oxford American magazine (the offices are upstairs), Chef Matthew Bell's re-envisioning of the space once utilized by longtime Main Street mainstay Juanita's Cantina has become a keystone in the revitalization of the neighborhood. He and his staff accomplish this with southern dishes, reimagined - pork meatballs with tomato gravy, chicken livers served over salad greens with bacon and buttermilk dressing, pickles, boiled peanuts. The restaurant's meatless burger is a nicely constructed answer, fusing Americana diner flavor with the garden, in the Hoppin' John Veggie Burger. Chef's black eyed pea and rice patty is accompanied by fresh greens, onions and pickled jalapeños and served with a smear of Crystal mayo and a side of fries.

1304 South Main Street, Little Rock
(501)244.9660 * SouthOnMain.com

PARALLADA JALISCO'Z
Taqueria Jalisco'z

Southwest Little Rock's Latino reinvention has brought a bevy of Mexican regional restaurants to town, offering an opportunity to taste the states of our southern neighbor in a series of dinners. Taqueria Jalisco'z parallada sizzler, a cast iron plate with a mixed grill of sausages, chicken breasts, steak, shrimp and peppers with sides is one of the best way to enjoy excellently prepared foods without busting your budget. The tacos are similarly grand.

5412 Baseline Road; Little Rock * (501) 753-4248
4718 Camp Robinson Road, North Little Rock * (501) 753-4248

113

FRIED MUSHROOMS
Wagon Wheel Restarant

Breakfast, lunch or dinner, there's a crowd at this Greenbrier family restaurant. They come in for plate lunch specials and country sides, catfish on Friday and big omelets for breakfast. Those in the know ask for these mushrooms, battered and fried in-house and served napalm hot with Ranch. Once you're done, check out what's in the pie case. Cream and meringue pies are almost always ready to slice, even lush concoctions like the banana split pie.

166 South Broadview Street, Greenbrier
(501) 679-5009

PETER RABBIT
WunderHaus

The evolution of the WunderBus food truck into a former classic gas station came with a pledge to merge European cuisine with Arkansas classics. The result is a marvelous space full of light, local food and good brews. The popular Peter Rabbit, a plate of roasted vegetable hash topped with an egg and a drizzle of housemade honey mustard marries together flavors into something particularly unique.

900 Locust Street, Conway
(501) 358-6806 * WunderHausConway.com

115

INDEX

This book would not be possible without the support of Arkansas's restaurant, hospitality and tourism industries, who work extraordinarily hard to ensure a good guest experience for visitors and locals alike.

Thank you to the Fort Smith Convention & Visitors Bureau, the Eureka Springs Advertising and Promotions Commission, the 1905 Basin Park Hotel, the West Memphis Convention & Visitors Bureau, Dogwood Hills Guest Farm, and King-Rhodes & Associates for assistance with lodging.

Gratitude to the Arkansas Educationsl Television Network for supporting the creation of this book.

A special thanks to Kerry Kraus for proofreading this book.

And to Hunter Robinson and Grav Weldon, who were patient and helpful while I worked on tandem compiling this book and the last and who put up with me while I put this book in motion.

Kat Robinson is Arkansas's food historian and most enthusiastic road warrior. The Little Rock-based travel writer is the host of the Emmy-nominated documentary *Make Room For Pie: A Delicious Slice of The Natural State* and a committee member for the Arkansas Food Hall of Fame. The author of *Arkansas Food: The A to Z of Eating in The Natural State* and *101 Things to Eat in Arkansas Before You Die*, Robinson has also compiled the comprehensive travel guide for pie lovers, *Another Slice of Arkansas Pie: A Guide to the Best Restaurants, Bakeries, Truck Stops and Food Trucks for Delectable Bites in The Natural State* (2018). Her other books are *Arkansas Pie: A Delicious Slice of the Natural State* (2012), *Classic Eateries of the Ozarks and Arkansas River Valley* (2013), and *Classic Eateries of the Arkansas Delta* (2014). She is the Arkansas fellow and curator to the National Food and Beverage Foundation, and the 2011 Arkansas Department of Parks and Tourism Henry Award winner for Media Support. With this book, *102 More Things to Eat in Arkansas Before You Die*, Robinson expands on the answer to the immediate question "where should I eat in Arkansas?"

Robinson's work appears in regional and national publications, websites and networks including *Food Network, Forbes Travel Guide, Serious Eats, AAA Magazines* and *AY Magazine*, among others. While she writes on food and travel subjects throughout the United States, she is best known for her ever-expanding knowledge of Arkansas food history and restaurant culture, all of which she explores on her 1200+ article website, *TieDyeTravels.com*. She lives with daughter Hunter and partner Grav Weldon in Little Rock.

For questions about Arkansas food or to reach the author, contact *kat@tiedyetravels.com*.

For more information on this book and others through Tonti Press, visit TontiPress.com.

CPSIA information can be obtained
at www.ICGtesting.com
Printed in the USA
LVHW012155260623
750818LV00007B/123